# HR APPROVED WAYS TO TELL COWORKERS THEY'RE STUPID

ELOF NYSTRON

This book  belongs to

## NTRODUCTION

# What I Really Want To Say:

I can't believe I'm dealing with this bullshit right now.

 HR Approved Alternative:

This situation certainly has it's challenges.

# What I Really Want To Say:

If you think I'm doing that crap, you're out of your damn mind.

 HR Approved Alternative:

That doesn't sound like it falls within my responsibilities.

# What I Really Want To Say:

I'm drowning in this shit storm you created.

 HR Approved Alternative:

This has become quite a challenging project to manage.

# What I Really Want To Say:

You seriously think I have time for this fucking nonsense?

 HR Approved Alternative:

My schedule is a bit tight at the moment.

# What I Really Want To Say:

**Who the hell thought this was a good idea?**

 HR Approved Alternative:

I'm curious to know the thought process behind this.

# What I Really Want To Say:

> **Oh, just fucking perfect, another last-minute change.**

 ## HR Approved Alternative:

I'll do my best to accommodate the recent update.

# What I Really Want To Say:

This is the stupidest fucking thing I've ever seen.

 HR Approved Alternative:

This approach may need some refining.

# What I Really Want To Say:

Great, another pointless fucking meeting.

 HR Approved Alternative:

Maybe a quick email summary could suffice next time.

# What I Really Want To Say:

Are you fucking serious with that request?

 HR Approved Alternative:

I'd love to understand more about your expectations here.

14

# What I Really Want To Say:

**I'm not your damn babysitter!**

 ## HR Approved Alternative:

I'd encourage you to try tackling this independently.

# What I Really Want To Say:

Why the hell am I doing everyone else's job?

 HR Approved Alternative:

It seems like we could distribute responsibilities more evenly.

# What I Really Want To Say:

If I hear one more stupid fucking idea, I might scream.

 HR Approved Alternative:

Let's try to prioritize actionable ideas.

# What I Really Want To Say:

For fucks sake, read the damn email.

 HR Approved Alternative:

Please refer to the email for more details.

# What I Really Want To Say:

**No, I don't want to stay late and fix your mess!**

 HR Approved Alternative:

I have some prior commitments after hours today.

# What I Really Want To Say:

I'm so done with this shit!

 HR Approved Alternative:

I'm feeling a bit overwhelmed at the moment.

# What I Really Want To Say:

That's some top-shelf bullshit right there.

 HR Approved Alternative:

That's an interesting perspective.

21

# What I Really Want To Say:

Can you please stop asking stupid fucking questions?

 HR Approved Alternative:

Let's stay solution-focused.

# What I Really Want To Say:

Oh sure, I'll just pull a miracle out of my ass.

## HR Approved Alternative:

I'll give it my best shot.

## What I Really Want To Say:

**Who the fuck died and made you boss?**

 HR Approved Alternative:

**Let's work together to get this resolved.**

What I Really Want To Say:

Holy shit, do you ever stop complaining?

 HR Approved Alternative:

I'm open to constructive feedback.

# What I Really Want To Say:

This is way above my pay grade of crap.

 HR Approved Alternative:

I'll reach out for support if needed.

# What I Really Want To Say:

I can't make your shit problem magically disappear.

 HR Approved Alternative:

I'm here to assist where I can.

# What I Really Want To Say:

You must be fucking kidding me with this.

 HR Approved Alternative:

Let's come up with a solid approach.

# What I Really Want To Say:

So we're going with your half-baked plan then, great.

 HR Approved Alternative:

We'll handle it one step at a time.

# What I Really Want To Say:

## Oh joy, another crisis I didn't create.

 HR Approved Alternative:

## This may require some teamwork.

# What I Really Want To Say:

Does anyone here actually do their fucking job?

 HR Approved Alternative:

Let's discuss this to make sure we're aligned.

# What I Really Want To Say:

Why the hell is this even a conversation?

 HR Approved Alternative:

I'll consider that suggestion.

# What I Really Want To Say:

i'm not saying you're the worst, but you're definitely not the best.

 HR Approved Alternative:

There's always room for growth and improvement. Let's work on reaching the next level.

# What I Really Want To Say:

You're like a cloud. When you disappear, it's a beautiful day.

 HR Approved Alternative:

I think we might work better independently on this task to maximize efficiency.

# What I Really Want To Say:

You're like a speed bump—slowing everything down for no reason.

 HR Approved Alternative:

We could explore ways to streamline our process for quicker results.

# What I Really Want To Say:

You're as bright as a black hole, and twice as dense

 HR Approved Alternative:

It seems we might be missing some key details. Let's review together to fill in the gaps.

# What I Really Want To Say:

Your elevator doesn't reach the top floor, does it?

 HR Approved Alternative:

There may be some areas of understanding we need to improve. Let's address those.

# What I Really Want To Say:

> **You're the human embodiment of a 404 error.**

 ## HR Approved Alternative:

It seems like there's a disconnect here. Let's troubleshoot and realign our focus to avoid confusion.

# What I Really Want To Say:

Oh, fantastic, another meeting that could've been summed up in a two-line email.

 HR Approved Alternative:

I think a quick email recap might be a more efficient option next time.

# What I Really Want To Say:

Oh, sure, let me just pull a brilliant idea out of my magic hat.

 HR Approved Alternative:

I'll brainstorm some creative solutions.

# What I Really Want To Say:

Just checking—do I have 'magician' in my job title? Because this feels like magic work.

 HR Approved Alternative:

I'll give it my best shot, though it may be challenging.

# What I Really Want To Say:

**Yep, I'll get right on that... right after I finish curing world hunger and achieving world peace.**

 HR Approved Alternative:

I'll add that to my list and work on it as soon as possible.

42

# What I Really Want To Say:

Ah, yes, another task with no clear purpose and no end in sight. My favorite kind.

 HR Approved Alternative:

I'd love some clarification on the end goals for this task.

# What I Really Want To Say:

**I don't mean to brag, but I'm running on three hours of sleep and caffeine fumes.**

 ## HR Approved Alternative:

I'm a bit tired today, but I'll give this my full attention.

# What I Really Want To Say:

Oh, good, another request to do the impossible with zero resources. I live for this!

 HR Approved Alternative:

It seems like this might be difficult with our current resources.

# What I Really Want To Say:

Yeah, no worries, I'll just clone myself to get that done faster.

 HR Approved Alternative:

I'll do my best to prioritize this, though I'm handling a few tasks right now.

# What I Really Want To Say:

**No problem, I'll be a mind-reader, a miracle worker, and an overachiever all at once!**

 HR Approved Alternative:

I'll do my best to find a solution, though it may take some time.

# What I Really Want To Say:

**So we're doing things with absolutely
no planning, no strategy?
Bold move.**

 HR Approved Alternative:

This may work better with some planning and structure.

# What I Really Want To Say:

Nothing says 'teamwork' like doing everything myself.

 HR Approved Alternative:

I'd appreciate any support from the team on this.

# What I Really Want To Say:

**Sure, I'll get it done right after I finish the fifty other urgent tasks I already have.**

 HR Approved Alternative:

I'll do my best to get this done, though my plate is quite full.

# What I Really Want To Say:

Oh, you wanted that done yesterday? Perfect, because I just invented a time machine.

 HR Approved Alternative:

It seems like there was a mix-up in timing, but I'll work on it now.

# What I Really Want To Say:

Why yes, I did go to college for this. Couldn't wait to make spreadsheets all day!

 HR Approved Alternative:

I'm putting my organizational skills to good use!

# What I Really Want To Say:

I'm not saying it's a bad idea, but it might be the worst idea I've ever heard.

 HR Approved Alternative:

Maybe we could consider a few alternative approaches here.

# What I Really Want To Say:

**Of course, I can get it done in no time! I'll just temporarily pause the space-time continuum.**

 ## HR Approved Alternative:

I'll make sure to get to it as soon as possible.

# What I Really Want To Say:

Oh, wonderful. Yet another fire drill to put out. My favorite!

 HR Approved Alternative:

This looks like it might need some immediate attention.

# What I Really Want To Say:

You're slower than a dial-up connection in 1999.

 HR Approved Alternative:

There's definitely an opportunity to improve our speed and efficiency moving forward.

## What I Really Want To Say:

I'm going to need about ten more cups of coffee before I'm ready for this.

 HR Approved Alternative:

I'll take a quick coffee break and get right to it.

## What I Really Want To Say:

Your brain is like a web browser —too many tabs open, none of them working.

 HR Approved Alternative:

It seems like there's a lot going on. Let's focus on prioritizing the most important tasks.

# What I Really Want To Say:

Oh, sure, let's just throw out the rule book and wing it!

 HR Approved Alternative:

A more structured approach might be beneficial here.

# What I Really Want To Say:

Another 30-minute meeting to cover what could've been a 2-second chat. Great use of time!

 ## HR Approved Alternative:

I think a quick discussion might work better for this.

# What I Really Want To Say:

I'm not sure if I should be impressed or concerned by your lack of competence.

 HR Approved Alternative:

It seems like there's some room for skill development here. Let's work on addressing that.

# What I Really Want To Say:

You remind me of a software update—always interrupting and never actually fixing anything.

 HR Approved Alternative:

Sometimes it's important to ensure our contributions are adding value rather than causing disruptions.

# What I Really Want To Say:

If stupidity were a currency, you'd be a billionaire.

 HR Approved Alternative:

There are definitely some opportunities for improvement that we can focus on to maximize your potential.

# What I Really Want To Say:

You're a walking argument for the invention of spell check.

 HR Approved Alternative:

Attention to detail is important. Let's work on ensuring accuracy moving forward.

64

# What I Really Want To Say:

You need that done in five minutes? Perfect, I'll just add superpowers to my resume.

 HR Approved Alternative:

I'll see what I can do within that timeframe.

# What I Really Want To Say:

You have the organizational skills of a tornado.

 HR Approved Alternative:

It might help to implement more structured organization techniques for better results.

66

# What I Really Want To Say:

Congratulations, you've set a new standard for mediocrity.

 HR Approved Alternative:

It's important that we continue to raise the bar and aim for higher standards.

# What I Really Want To Say:

**If ignorance is bliss, you must be the happiest person alive.**

 HR Approved Alternative:

Gaining more knowledge and staying informed can definitely help us reach better outcomes.

# What I Really Want To Say:

Are you intentionally this dumb, or is it just a talent?

 HR Approved Alternative:

Let's work on improving our problem-solving strategies to prevent these issues in the future.

# What I Really Want To Say:

How do you manage to screw up so consistently? It's almost impressive.

 HR Approved Alternative:

We can learn from these mistakes to ensure more consistent performance moving forward.

What I Really Want To Say:

I'd suggest you go outside and get some fresh air, but I don't think nature can fix that.

 HR Approved Alternative:

Sometimes a break can provide a fresh perspective, but we also need to focus on the root cause of the issue.

# What I Really Want To Say:

Great idea. Let's all just ignore logic and reason completely.

 HR Approved Alternative:

Maybe we should evaluate the pros and cons of this approach.

What I Really Want To Say:

Yep, that's exactly how I'd do it
if I were trying to make
everything ten times harder.

 HR Approved Alternative:

Perhaps a different approach could
streamline this process.

# What I Really Want To Say:

Oh sure, why don't I just stay all night? Who needs sleep, anyway?

 ## HR Approved Alternative:

I'll work on this as efficiently as I can.

# What I Really Want To Say:

Sure, I'll add that to the list of things that don't make any sense.

 HR Approved Alternative:

I'll do my best to incorporate this feedback.

# What I Really Want To Say:

No, please, keep talking. I wasn't listening to begin with.

 HR Approved Alternative:

I'll take notes to make sure I'm fully informed.

# What I Really Want To Say:

You're like a Wi-Fi signal in a storm—completely unreliable

 HR Approved Alternative:

Consistency is important. Let's find ways to ensure more dependable contributions in the future.

# What I Really Want To Say:

You're proof that the lights are on, but nobody's home.

 HR Approved Alternative:

There are times when clarity of focus is needed. Let's work on improving that together.

# What I Really Want To Say:

Oh, you're the expert now? How many minutes of experience do you have in this again?

 HR Approved Alternative:

It's great to see your enthusiasm. I'd be interested in hearing more about the ideas you're bringing from your experiences.

## What I Really Want To Say:

Wow, you've cracked the code of how to do absolutely nothing and call it work.

 HR Approved Alternative:

It's impressive how you've found ways to simplify tasks. Efficiency is something we can all continue to improve.

# What I Really Want To Say:

Oh, thanks for that feedback! I'll file it right next to my complete indifference.

 HR Approved Alternative:

Thank you for your feedback; I'll review it and consider how I can incorporate it moving forward.

# What I Really Want To Say:

Let me get this straight: you created the problem, and now I get to solve it?

 HR Approved Alternative:

I'm here to help resolve this issue. Let's work together to prevent similar situations in the future.

## What I Really Want To Say:

Wow, that's a revolutionary idea— I'm shocked no one else has thought of it.

 ## HR Approved Alternative:

Thank you for the suggestion. It's always good to revisit ideas, even ones that may have been considered previously.

# What I Really Want To Say:

Yes, because adding more people to the call always speeds things up.

 HR Approved Alternative:

I appreciate the team approach. If we'd like to streamline the process, perhaps we can focus on those directly involved.

# What I Really Want To Say:

Oh, I'm thrilled to hear about your vacation again. Truly, it's a highlight of my day.

 HR Approved Alternative:

Sounds like you had a great time! I'll catch up with you later—I need to focus on this project right now.

# What I Really Want To Say:

I would love to help you with your job–again–but I have my own to do.

 ## HR Approved Alternative:

I can assist you briefly, but to stay on track with my own deadlines, I may need to hand this back to you soon.

# What I Really Want To Say:

**Oh good, another brilliant idea with zero thought behind it.**

 HR Approved Alternative:

Interesting concept! Let's take a few minutes to go over any potential implications before we move forward.

# What I Really Want To Say:

**Right, because nothing says 'effective team' like eight people doing the same thing.**

 ## HR Approved Alternative:

I appreciate the focus on teamwork. To avoid overlap, maybe we can assign specific roles to each person.

# What I Really Want To Say:

Perfect! I didn't want any free time tonight anyway.

 HR Approved Alternative:

I'll do my best to prioritize this task while balancing it with my other responsibilities.

# What I Really Want To Say:

Oh, you 'forgot'? How shocking and completely out of character!

 HR Approved Alternative:

I understand; things slip our minds. Let's put a reminder in place to help prevent this in the future.

# What I Really Want To Say:

I'd love to explain it for the fifth time—it's my favorite pastime.

 HR Approved Alternative:

I'm happy to clarify. I'll make a note in case we need to revisit this later as well.

# What I Really Want To Say:

You're right—let's make it overly complicated for no apparent reason.

 HR Approved Alternative:

I see where you're going. Let's try to balance thoroughness with simplicity for efficiency.

# What I Really Want To Say:

I can tell by your emails you definitely have a PhD in nagging.

 HR Approved Alternative:

Thank you for the reminders; I understand the importance. I'll make sure to keep you updated.

# What I Really Want To Say:

You're as reliable as a flip phone in 2024.

 HR Approved Alternative:

Consistency and reliability are key. Let's work on improving those aspects moving forward.

What I Really Want To Say:

**I'm absolutely dying to hear more about this groundbreaking suggestion of yours.**

 HR Approved Alternative:

I'd like to understand more about your perspective. Could you elaborate on what led you to this idea?

# What I Really Want To Say:

Amazing, you've solved a problem I didn't even have.

 HR Approved Alternative:

Thank you for your input. I hadn't identified that as an issue, but I'll keep it in mind going forward.

# What I Really Want To Say:

Brilliant! Another decision based on nothing but vibes.

 HR Approved Alternative:

It would be helpful to discuss the reasoning behind this approach to ensure we're aligned with our objectives.

# What I Really Want To Say:

Ah, you've come to save the day with your incredible lack of expertise!

 HR Approved Alternative:

I appreciate your willingness to help. Let's work together to make sure all perspectives are considered.

# What I Really Want To Say:

**Wonderful, more unnecessary tasks. This is definitely my life's purpose.**

 HR Approved Alternative:

I appreciate the additional tasks; I'll make sure to prioritize effectively to keep things moving smoothly.

# What I Really Want To Say:

Another meeting to talk about nothing? Can't wait!

 HR Approved Alternative:

I look forward to the discussion and will prepare some talking points to make sure our time is productive.

# What I Really Want To Say:

Oh, goody, another 'urgent' task that's going to be forgotten by tomorrow.

 HR Approved Alternative:

Thanks for the heads-up on this priority. I'll work on it promptly and keep you posted.

# What I Really Want To Say:

Amazing! Your lack of attention to detail is really an art form.

 HR Approved Alternative:

Attention to detail is always helpful. Let's work together to make sure nothing slips through.

## What I Really Want To Say:

Oh, so that's the plan now? Glad I was finally looped in at the last second.

 HR Approved Alternative:

Thank you for the update. If possible, let's coordinate earlier next time for smoother execution.

# What I Really Want To Say:

Another meeting about nothing? How did I get so lucky?

 HR Approved Alternative:

I'm looking forward to staying aligned as a team. Let's keep it focused so we can maximize our time.

What I Really Want To Say:

You know, chaos seems to be our primary strategy here.

 HR Approved Alternative:

We have a lot of moving parts. Let's work on creating a clear, manageable plan moving forward.

# What I Really Want To Say:

Glad you think my job is just clicking buttons all day.

 HR Approved Alternative:

There's more complexity to this than it may seem. I'm happy to clarify if it's helpful.

# What I Really Want To Say:

Wow, you actually read my email? It's a miracle!

 HR Approved Alternative:

Thanks for your prompt attention to my message. I'm here if you have any follow-up questions.

# What I Really Want To Say:

Another untested idea,
thrown together last minute?
This should be fun.

 HR Approved Alternative:

Let's make sure we allow time for a
proper review so we can address
any unforeseen challenges.

# What I Really Want To Say:

Amazing—another complex problem caused by your inability to plan.

 HR Approved Alternative:

Let's tackle this issue and work on creating strategies to avoid similar situations.

## What I Really Want To Say:

**Oh, more office gossip. I'm riveted.**

 HR Approved Alternative:

I'm here to support our team culture. Let's focus on ways to stay productive together.

## What I Really Want To Say:

Oh, you're putting me in charge? Great, because I didn't already have a mountain of work.

 HR Approved Alternative:

I'm honored to take this on. I'll prioritize it among my current tasks and keep you updated.

## What I Really Want To Say:

**Sure, I'll just magically pull that from thin air. No biggie.**

 ## HR Approved Alternative:

I'll get creative and see what solutions I can develop to meet this need.

# What I Really Want To Say:

I'd love to hear more of your 'genius' ideas, but unfortunately, I only have 24 hours in a day.

 ## HR Approved Alternative:

Let's discuss our priorities to ensure we're making the most of our time.

# What I Really Want To Say:

**Oh, you 'forgot' to tell me again? Classic.**

 HR Approved Alternative:

I understand things can slip through. I'd appreciate being kept in the loop for smoother planning.

# What I Really Want To Say:

Just what I needed—a new project with zero resources and an impossible deadline.

 HR Approved Alternative:

I'll make the most of our available resources to get this project moving forward.

# What I Really Want To Say:

**Wonderful. Another meeting that could've been a two-sentence email.**

 HR Approved Alternative:

I'm looking forward to our discussion. Let's aim to keep it efficient.

## What I Really Want To Say:

Oh, a new corporate initiative? Let me grab my pom-poms and fake enthusiasm.

 ## HR Approved Alternative:

I'll approach this new initiative with a positive outlook and give it my full support.

# What I Really Want To Say:

Another spreadsheet? How exciting! My soul feels alive.

 HR Approved Alternative:

Thanks for providing this data. I'll dive into the details and get back to you.

# What I Really Want To Say:

Brilliant idea—adding more chaos to the chaos. Genius move.

 HR Approved Alternative:

It seems like a more streamlined approach could be beneficial here. I'd be happy to suggest options that might keep us on track.

# What I Really Want To Say:

Oh, don't worry, I'm just a robot with infinite energy!

 HR Approved Alternative:

I'll prioritize this with the resources I have.

# What I Really Want To Say:

Oh, fantastic! More 'urgent' crap that could've been an email!

 HR Approved Alternative:

I'm on it! Let's tackle these priorities one at a time.

## What I Really Want To Say:

**Oh, so I'm the one holding this all together? Awesome. Maybe give me a raise next time.**

 ## HR Approved Alternative:

Glad to help out where I can—let me know if there's room for growth!

# What I Really Want To Say:

**Wow, a third meeting on this today? Nothing like beating a dead horse for fun.**

 HR Approved Alternative:

Let's keep this focused so we can make the most of our time.

# What I Really Want To Say:

Oh yeah, now it's my problem.
Got it.

 HR Approved Alternative:

I'll take a look and see how I can
help move this forward.

# What I Really Want To Say:

Because that's exactly what I needed—more BS on my plate!

 HR Approved Alternative:

Thanks for keeping me in the loop. I'll see how I can reprioritize.

# What I Really Want To Say:

I can definitely read your mind; just give me a second to find my crystal ball.

 HR Approved Alternative:

Could you clarify that a bit more? I want to make sure we're aligned.

# What I Really Want To Say:

Another completely useless meeting? Sign me the hell up!

 HR Approved Alternative:

Thanks for the invite! I'll be there with my thoughts.

## What I Really Want To Say:

Another completely useless meeting? Sign me the hell up!

 HR Approved Alternative:

Thanks for the invite! I'll be there with my thoughts.

# What I Really Want To Say:

**So happy to play cleanup for everyone else's screw-ups!**

 HR Approved Alternative:

I'll look into it and help however I can to keep us on track.

# What I Really Want To Say:

Wow, another training session on common sense. Can't wait.

 HR Approved Alternative:

I'll be there and look forward to learning something new.

Made in United States
Troutdale, OR
12/15/2024